Dear Little Me,

Dear Little Me,

written & illustrated by Emmanuel E. Hanson

dear reader,

this book is meant to get you back into the mind of little you — the you that had to handle big scary things that you didn't have the tools to deal with yet. the you that is scared that living your life will make it fall apart. so close your eyes and imagine that — wait no. this is a book and you might need your eyes to read. dont close your eyes, and imagine that you are having a conversation with little you.

Dear little me,

I know you weren't ready for everything to change.

I know that everything fell apart.

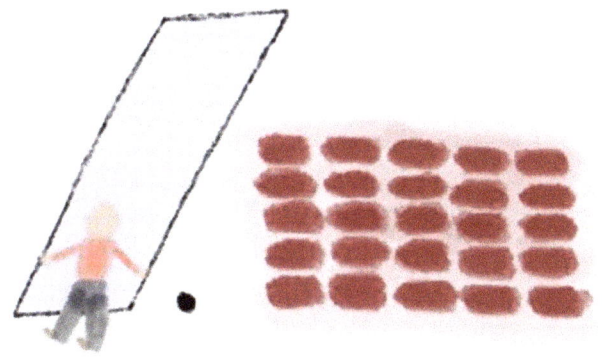

I know you had to clean things up all on your own

and when you had cleaned up the mess

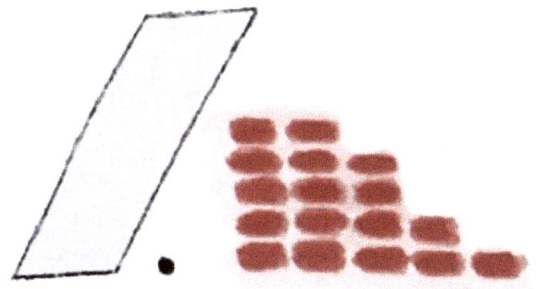

you had to rebuild it

all by yourself.

but you didn't have any tools

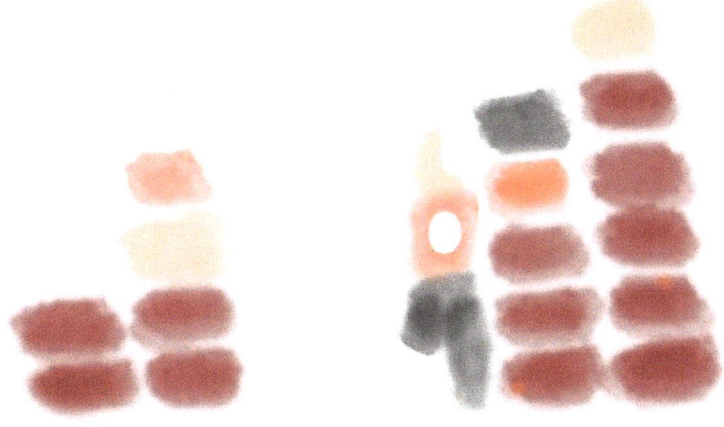

so you used pieces of yourself instead

and when you had rebuilt it

you had to fight

to keep it
from being torn apart again.

and though you survived all that,
you're so tired now

that everything is hard.

but you're also a little bigger now

which means you can find some tools
you weren't tall enough to reach before

and even though things still seem scary and big

you can start to get pieces of yourself back

that you haven't seen

in a long time

and you might need some help to do that

and that's okay.

it doesn't mean you aren't

smart

or strong

or brave

quite the opposite actually

you're all of those things

and you might still feel alone

but you have a better support system now

and if you don't,
you have the option to create one

and no matter what,
I will be there to hold your hand

just like I was
when we were small.

so little me,
it's going to be okay.

Love,
Less little you ♡

Author's Note

Hi! My name is Emmanuel Hanson.

I wrote this book as a letter to my younger self – the me who had to grow up too fast, the me who took care of herself because there was no one else to do it for her, and the me who still hurts every time she is described as resilient. I hope this book is as healing for you to read as it was for me to write.

Interestingly enough, I never planned to write a book. I simply woke up one day with the idea for "Dear Little Me," in my head and needed to put it on paper. So, at a local coffee shop, I sat down and hand scrawled the entirety of this book in about two hours (yes, the handwriting in this book is the original manuscript).

Over the course of the next several months, the illustrations came to life, until finally, we come to this point – you holding this book in your hands. I am so excited for the release of my first book, and cannot wait to see the impact it has on the people who read it. Thank you for being one of them!

p.s. this book was officially approved by my therapist

Copyright © 2026
Emmanuel Hanson, Author & Illustrator
Publisher: Thy Name, Inc. (McLean, VA)

Rights and Permissions: All rights reserved. No portion of this book may be reproduced, stored in a retrieval system, or transmitted in any form or by any means — electronic, mechanical, photocopy, recording, scanning, or other — except for brief cited quotations in critical reviews or articles, without prior written permission of the publisher.

ISBN: 978-1-967283-00-2 (HC)
Printed in USA

THY NAME
Publishing

Thy-Name.com

www.ingramcontent.com/pod-product-compliance
Lightning Source LLC
Chambersburg PA
CBHW062022050526
44107CB00106B/954